THE
MAGNIFICENT
❖ BOOK ❖
OF
BIRDS

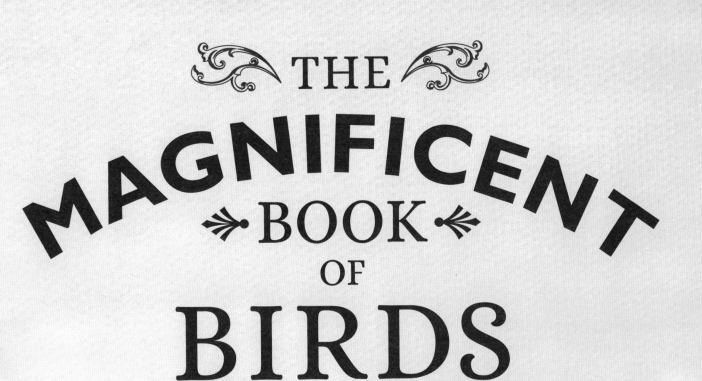

THE MAGNIFICENT BOOK OF BIRDS

ILLUSTRATED BY
Val Walerczuk

WRITTEN BY
Tom Jackson

Published by Weldon Owen Children's Books
An imprint of Weldon Owen International, L.P.
A subsidiary of Insight International, L.P.
PO Box 3088
San Rafael, CA 94912
www.insighteditions.com

Additional illustrations: Simon Mendez
Senior Editor: Diana Craig
Editorial Coordinator: Pandita Geary
Designers: Tom Forge & Emma Forge
Consultant: Kim Bryan
Creative Director: Bryn Walls
Publisher: Sue Grabham

Insight Editions:
Publisher: Raoul Goff

Manufactured, printed, and assembled in Turkey.
Second printing, October 2021, Levent. LVT1021.

23 22 21 2 3 4 5

ISBN: 978-1-68188-768-5

Introduction

Birds are at home in every corner of the world, from the wide-open ocean and frozen tundra to the lush jungles of the tropics. They are also seen in urban spaces, in gardens, parks, and city streets. There are about 10,000 types, or species, of bird living today, and they have been evolving since prehistoric times. These elegant descendants of dinosaurs have been soaring through the skies for more than 100 million years.

The Magnificent Book of Birds introduces you to some of the most glorious species, including the largest, the smallest, the fastest, and the longest-lived, as well as the toughest bird of all, the emperor penguin. This is the only animal to live through winter on Antarctica and survive to see the next summer. You'll also meet some amazing species such as an eagle that eats monkeys and seabirds that can sleep while flying over the ocean. Find out how one parrot makes itself a loudspeaker to boost the sound of its booming calls and why another nibbles on clay.

Get to know all these magnificent and fascinating birds as you travel the world's forests, seas, and skies.

Fact file

Lives: New Guinea and northeastern Australia

Habitat: Rainforest

Length: 4¼–5½ ft (1.3–1.7 m)

Wingspan: Just a few feathers

Weight: 64–128 lb (29–58 kg)

Lifespan: 30 years

Diet: Fallen fruit, fungi, small animals, carrion

 # Contents

Raggiana bird of paradise

Paradisaea raggiana

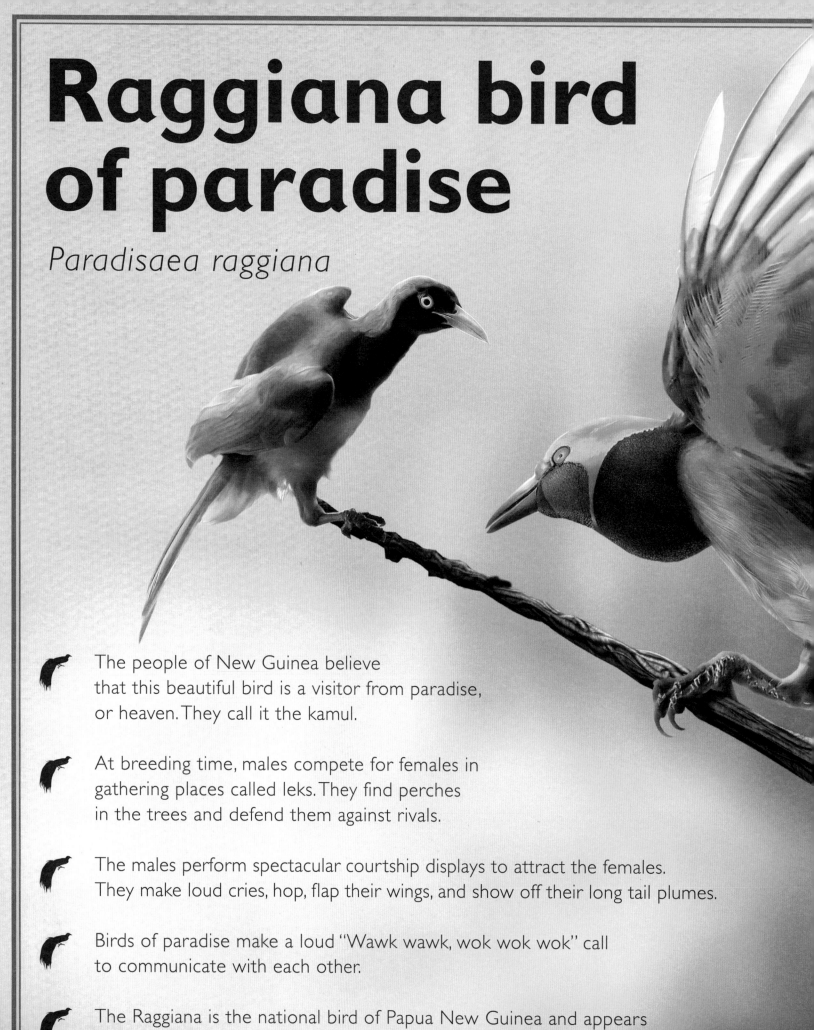

- The people of New Guinea believe that this beautiful bird is a visitor from paradise, or heaven. They call it the kamul.

- At breeding time, males compete for females in gathering places called leks. They find perches in the trees and defend them against rivals.

- The males perform spectacular courtship displays to attract the females. They make loud cries, hop, flap their wings, and show off their long tail plumes.

- Birds of paradise make a loud "Wawk wawk, wok wok wok" call to communicate with each other.

- The Raggiana is the national bird of Papua New Guinea and appears on the country's flag.

Fact file

Lives: Indonesia and New Guinea

Habitat: Lowland and hill forest

Length: 13¾–17¾ in (35–45 cm)

Wingspan: 24 in (60 cm)

Weight: 6 oz (170 g)

Lifespan: 7 years

Diet: Fruits, berries, insects, spiders, centipedes, millipedes

Toco toucan

Ramphastos toco

- The toco toucan's enormous beak is hollow inside. It has a structure like a honeycomb, which stops it from being too heavy.

- The toucan uses its long, bristly tongue to find insects in cracks in wood. It flicks them up with its beak so they fall straight into its throat.

- Toucans have small wings, so they are not good at flying. They hop from branch to branch collecting food, then flap a short distance to reach the next tree.

- When it feels hot, the toucan pumps blood into its hollow beak. This helps the bird to cool down.

- Every year toucans court one another by throwing fruit into each other's mouths.

- Toucans lay their eggs in tree trunks, in old, empty nests that once belonged to woodpeckers.

- The beak of a toucan chick will not reach full size for several months, and its colorful patterns will not be fully developed until nearly one year.

Fact file

Lives: South America

Habitat: Savannah and woodland

Length: 22–24 in (55–61 cm)

Wingspan: 47 in (119 cm)

Weight: 1–2 lb (500–860 g)

Lifespan: 20 years

Diet: Fruit, insects, birds' eggs, chicks, lizards

Philippine eagle

Pithecophaga jefferyi

- The Philippine eagle is the largest eagle in the world.

- This eagle lives on four islands in the northeast Philippines. It nests in the rainforest, near the tops of the mountains.

- The Phillippine eagle was once called the monkey-eating eagle because people thought it only ate monkeys. It is just as likely to eat bats, squirrels, birds, reptiles, and even small deer.

- The eagle has long, brown feathers on the back of its neck that form a shaggy crest. It can raise this crest to make it look fierce.

- High up in the trees, the eagle looks for prey, then swoops down to grab the victim with its talons. It kills the prey by ripping it with its huge hooked beak.

Fact file

Lives: Northeast Philippines

Habitat: Rainforest

Length: 35–40 in (90–100 cm)

Wingspan: 6–7 ft (1.84–2.2 m)

Weight: 10–17½ lb (4.5–8 kg)

Lifespan: 40 years

Diet: Monkeys, small mammals, bats, birds, reptiles

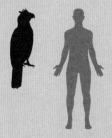

Phillippine eagles pair for life. They perform elaborate displays to impress their partners.

In one mating ritual, the male swoops up behind the female and shows off his talons. The female then spins around and flies upside down to display hers.

13

Scarlet macaw

Ara macao

- This macaw is the world's largest parrot, with tail feathers that are almost as long as its body.

- Like all parrots, the scarlet macaw has a thick, hooked beak, which it uses to slice into fruits, crack open nutshells, and preen its feathers.

- In the wild, macaws mimic each other's calls and the sounds around them. When they live with humans, they learn to copy what people say.

- During the day, macaws look for food in the high branches of the rainforest. At night, they huddle together in the trees to avoid being attacked by snakes, monkeys, and other predators.

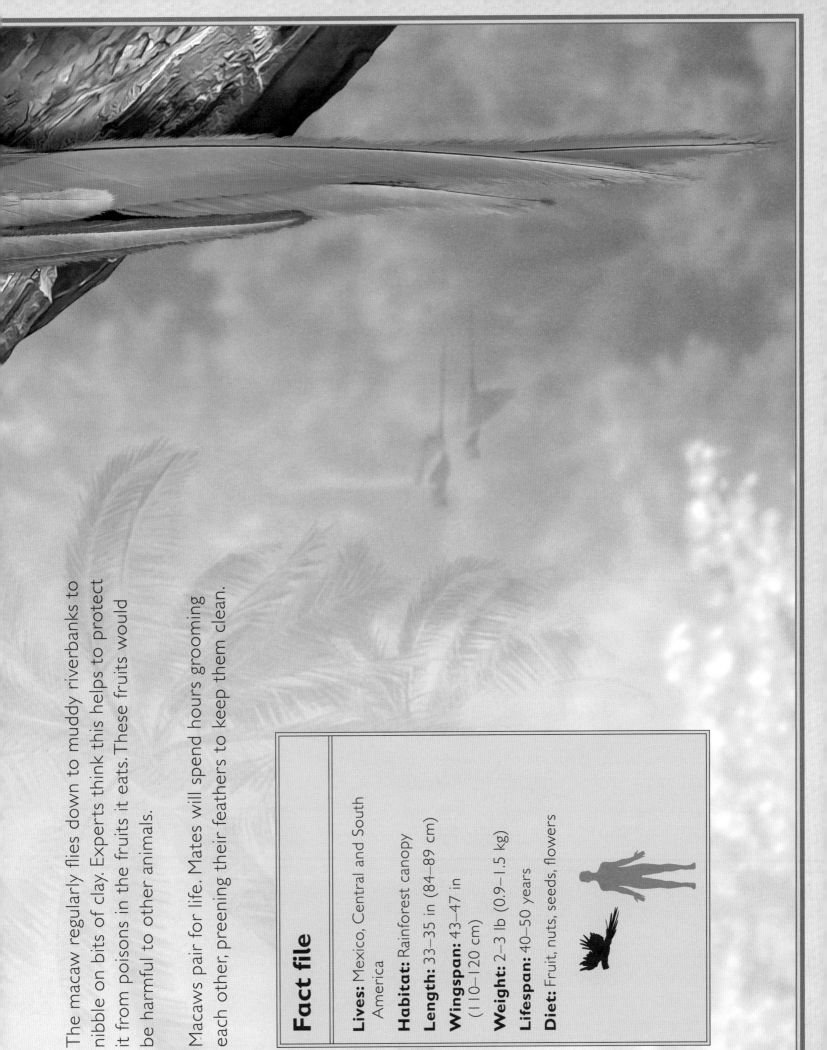

The macaw regularly flies down to muddy riverbanks to nibble on bits of clay. Experts think this helps to protect it from poisons in the fruits it eats. These fruits would be harmful to other animals.

Macaws pair for life. Mates will spend hours grooming each other, preening their feathers to keep them clean.

Fact file

Lives: Mexico, Central and South America

Habitat: Rainforest canopy

Length: 33–35 in (84–89 cm)

Wingspan: 43–47 in (110–120 cm)

Weight: 2–3 lb (0.9–1.5 kg)

Lifespan: 40–50 years

Diet: Fruit, nuts, seeds, flowers

Tufted puffin

Fratercula cirrhata

The tufted puffin spends most of its time far out at sea. It comes onto land only in spring to nest and lay a single egg.

Out at sea, puffins are usually solitary birds, but they may also live in pairs.

The tufted puffin hunts by swooping down to the surface of the ocean searching for prey. Then it dives down into large shoals of fish to snatch up food with its sturdy beak.

This skilled diver can stay underwater for a whole minute. It can dive down 80 ft (24 m) to grab crabs or other prey on the seabed.

The puffin catches fish one by one, using its tongue to press each fish against spines in the roof of its mouth. This holds the prey firmly in place while it opens its beak to scoop up the next catch.

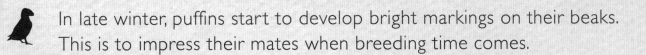 In late winter, puffins start to develop bright markings on their beaks. This is to impress their mates when breeding time comes.

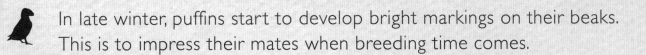 Puffins return to breed in the place they were born, often on an island away from predators.

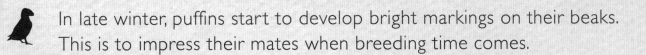 The birds lay one egg each year in a rock crevice or a burrow in the soil. The burrow may be 2–7 ft (60–200 cm) long.

Fact file

Lives: Northern Pacific Ocean

Habitat: Ocean, or grassy slopes and rocky clifftops

Length: 14–16 in (36–41 cm)

Wingspan: 25–26 in (64–66 cm)

Weight: 1–2 lb (0.52–1 kg)

Lifespan: 20 years

Diet: Fish, squid, crustaceans

Southern masked weaver

Ploceus velatus

🐦 The southern masked weaver has a short, chunky beak, which is strong enough to crack seeds.

🐦 The male weaver changes color to attact a mate. His feathers turn bright yellow and a dark patch that looks like a mask appears on his face.

🐦 To impress the female, the male builds her an elaborate nest. He starts with just a loop of grass hanging from a twig. He keeps adding grass stalks until the nest is shaped like a ball.

🐦 The weaver's nest has two chambers—a warm one in the middle for nighttime, and another near the entrance to give shade on hot days.

🐦 To attract a female, the male hangs from the bottom of the finished nest, clinging on with his long toes and singing, fanning his wings, and spreading his tail.

🐦 The male may make up to 25 nests each year to attract several different mates.

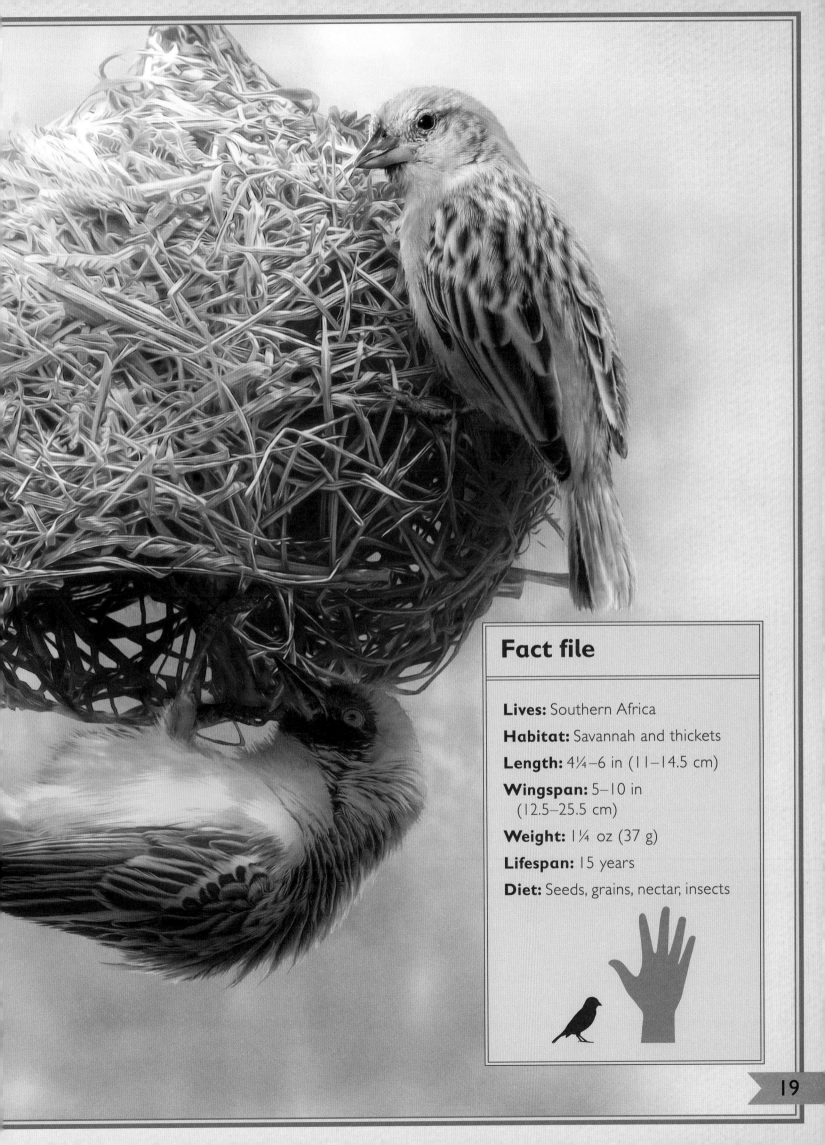

Fact file

Lives: Southern Africa

Habitat: Savannah and thickets

Length: 4¼–6 in (11–14.5 cm)

Wingspan: 5–10 in
(12.5–25.5 cm)

Weight: 1¼ oz (37 g)

Lifespan: 15 years

Diet: Seeds, grains, nectar, insects

Southern cassowary

Casuarius casuarius

This giant bird lives in the dense undergrowth on the rainforest floor. It cannot fly but walks slowly and quietly through the bushes.

The cassowary feeds mostly on the ripe fruits that fall from the trees above. It also eats fungi and insects, and may even gobble up lizards or frogs.

Cassowaries live alone. They make low, booming rumblings to warn other cassowaries to stay away. These calls are sometimes too deep for humans to hear.

Fact file

Lives: New Guinea and northeastern Australia

Habitat: Rainforest

Length: 4¼–5½ ft (1.3–1.7 m)

Wingspan: Just a few feathers

Weight: 64–128 lb (29–58 kg)

Lifespan: 30 years

Diet: Fallen fruit, fungi, small animals, carrion

The birds have strong legs for running away, but they may also stand and fight. Leaping feet-first at attackers, they slash at them with their razor-sharp claws.

After mating, the female lays her eggs in a nest that the male has made. Then she may go off to find her next mate while the male stays to look after the eggs.

The cassowary has a casque—a hollow crest of bone—on its head. This may help to make its calls boom even more loudly.

Emperor penguin

Aptenodytes forsteri

- The emperor is the biggest, heaviest penguin of all. This tough bird is also the only penguin to stay in Antarctica throughout the winter.

- Penguins use their wings as flippers to swim. Emperors can stay underwater for more than fifteen minutes at a time and dive to over 1640 ft (500 m), which is like diving from the top of a tall skyscraper.

- The penguins hunt at sea all summer, in preparation for breeding time in winter. The males will not eat all winter because they have to care for the chicks.

- As winter approaches, emperor penguins march nonstop, up to 70 miles (113 kilometres) across the snow and ice to breed.

- Male penguins look after the eggs, balancing them on their feet under a warm patch of skin on their bellies. The eggs must not roll away or they will freeze.

- In the Antarctic winter, the sun does not come up for weeks. As the temperature drops to −76°F (−60°C), hundreds of male penguins huddle together for warmth.

- Penguin families recognize each other by their calls, even in all the noise of the colony.

Fact file

Lives: Southern Ocean and Antarctica

Habitat: Polar ocean

Length: 45–48 in (115–122 cm)

Weight: 48½–99 lb (22–45 kg)

Lifespan: 20 years

Diet: Fish, crabs, squid

American white pelican

Pelecanus erythrorhynchos

 This pelican's beak is up to 14 in (36.5 cm) long, which is one of the longest of any bird. The top is flat but the underside is a pouch of stretchy skin.

 To catch its food, the bird scoops up water into its beak while swimming. The underside swells to hold the water and whatever food it contains.

 The bird's full beak holds about three times as much as its stomach. To empty it, the pelican carefully leans forward. The water inside the beak pours out and only the food is left.

Fact file

Lives: North America

Habitat: Freshwater rivers and lakes, coastal bays and inlets

Length: 4–6 ft (1.27–1.78 m)

Wingspan: 8–10 ft (2.44–2.99 m)

Weight: 11–18¾ lb (5–8.5 kg)

Lifespan: 16 years

Diet: Fish, amphibians, crayfish

Several pelicans work together to herd a shoal of fish into shallow water, where it is easier to scoop them up.

This pelican does not dive for food, but its feathers can get wet when it rains heavily. To dry them, it perches on the shore with its wings held out.

There are pockets of air trapped in the fatty skin under the bird's body. These may act like a life jacket to help the pelican stay afloat more easily.

Great horned owl

Bubo virginianus

- This bird is one of the largest of all owl species.

- The "horns" on the great horned owl's head are really feathery tufts. They help it to blend in with the gray-brown bark as it perches on a branch.

- The horned owl hunts at night by listening for the faint rustles of prey in the darkness. The feathers around its eyes gather sound waves and direct them to the owl's ears.

- The great horned owl can swoop down on prey in almost complete silence. The soft feathers in its wings help the owl to fly very quietly.

- The owl makes different calls to send different messages. A soft "hoo-hoo" is a warning to stay out of its hunting territory.

 During their mating ritual, great horned owls nod and bow to each other. They pair for life and raise their owlets together.

Fact file

Lives: North America, Mexico, Central and South America

Habitat: Woodland and forest, mangroves, deserts, farmlands

Length: 17¾–24 in (45–60 cm)

Wingspan: 36–60 in (91–152 cm)

Weight: 2–5½ lb (0.9–2.5 kg)

Lifespan: 25 years

Diet: Small mammals, birds, reptiles, amphibians, fish, insects

King eider

Somateria spectabilis

 The king eider lives along Arctic coastlines. In winter, the coastal sea freezes solid and the eider moves out onto the Arctic Ocean in flocks of 100,000 birds.

 To find food, the king eider dives to the seabed to snap up sea urchins, snails, clams, and crabs.

In spring, the Arctic coastlines thaw. The birds fly in from the sea and feed on plants and insects in shallow ponds and pools.

The king eider is a fast flier. It can reach speeds of 40 mph (64 km/h).

The male has bright plumage to show himself off to the females. The female has brown feathers to hide her from predators while she incubates her eggs.

In June, the female scrapes a hollow in the ground near a pond. She lines it with feathers and grass and lays her eggs there. She will not eat for three weeks until the eggs hatch.

Fact file

Lives: Arctic coasts of Europe, Asia and North America

Habitat: Ocean and inland tundra

Length: 17–25 in (43–63 cm)

Wingspan: 34–40 in (86–102 cm)

Weight: 2½–4½ lb (1.1–2 kg)

Lifespan: 15–20 years

Diet: Shellfish, insects, seeds, plants

California condor

Gymnogyps californianus

- The condor is one of the largest birds in North America. It has a wingspan of almost 10 ft (3 m).

- Huge wings allow condors to soar in the sky for long periods. They can stay in the air for hours at a time and travel more than 124 miles (200 km) a day to find food.

- The condor eats carrion, which is the flesh of dead animals. It can push its whole head into a carcass to feed.

- Condors reproduce slowly. They are not ready to breed until they are 6–8 years old, and the female lays only one egg at a time. If she successfully lays an egg, the pair won't breed again the following year.

- In 1987, there were only 27 wild condors left. Pesticides once used by farmers made it hard for the birds to lay healthy eggs.

Humans have been taking over the natural habitat, or wild spaces, where condors live. To help save the species, the last few wild birds were captured.

Conservationists (people who protect wildlife) are breeding captive condors and releasing them into the wild. This is slowly helping to increase condor numbers.

Fact file

Lives: North America, Mexico

Habitat: Wooded hills and shrubland near rocky cliffs

Length: 3½–4¼ ft (1.09–1.34 m)

Wingspan: 8–10 ft (2.49–3 m)

Weight: 18–31 lb (8–14 kg)

Lifespan: 45 years

Diet: Carrion

Painted bunting

Passerina ciris

- A Native American legend tells how all the birds waited in turn to be given their colors. The bunting was last in line so had to take dabs of whatever colors were left.

- When the male bunting reaches one year old, his green feathers start changing. They turn dazzling shades of red, blue, and green, as if they have been painted.

- Female and younger buntings have soft green plumage. Their coloring helps them to stay hidden in the woods where they live, safe from predators such as snakes.

- Painted buntings breed from April to August. The female builds a nest among tall grasses made from plant stems, grass stalks and scraps of animal hair.

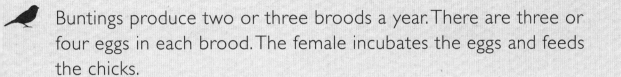 Buntings produce two or three broods a year. There are three or four eggs in each brood. The female incubates the eggs and feeds the chicks.

Male buntings defend their territory from rivals. They call out, attack intruders, and scare them off by slowly fluttering through the air like a butterfly.

During winter, the painted bunting pecks at seeds scattered on the ground. In summer, the bird eats insects as well.

Fact file

Lives: North and Central America

Habitat: Woodlands and bushes

Length: 4¾–5½ in (12–14 cm)

Wingspan: 8–8½ in (20–22 cm)

Weight: ½–¾ oz (13–19 g)

Lifespan: 10 years

Diet: Seeds, spiders, insects, snails

Great frigatebird

Fregata minor

- This seabird has to spend most of its time in the air. Its feathers are not waterproof and its short legs and small feet make swimming and walking difficult.

- A frigatebird's wingspan is a massive 7 ft (2.2 m). This allows it to soar almost effortlessly on the breeze for hours.

- The bird's forked tail helps it to steer in the air and to do quick turns.

- The frigatebird hunts during the day, snatching flying fish from the air and the sea, and stealing food from other seabirds.

- On calm nights, the frigatebird returns to roost on rocky cliffs. But when the weather is windy, it sleeps on the wing, floating on the air like a kite.

Fact file

Lives: Tropical and subtropical parts of the Pacific and Indian Oceans

Habitat: Warm seas, mangroves, islands

Length: 32–41 in (82–105 cm)

Wingspan: 6–7½ ft (1.8–2.3 m)

Weight: 2–3½ lb (1–1.6 kg)

Lifespan: 35 years

Diet: Fish, squid, eggs, chicks, baby turtles, carrion

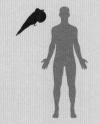

The female frigatebird is slightly larger than the male and has a white breast. The male is greenish-black but has a red air sac dangling from his throat. He can blow it up with air like a balloon.

At breeding time, the males compete for mates. They puff up their air sacs, spread their wings and make drumming sounds with their beaks. The females fly overhead to choose their partner.

35

Greater flamingo

Phoenicopterus roseus

 Flamingoes feed on microscopic creatures that live in salty water. The water passes through a hairy sieve inside their curved beaks, which filters out the food.

 The greater flamingo feeds with its head hanging upside-down in the water. It wiggles the upper part of its beak into the mud to loosen the food buried there.

 The feathers of the adult bird are really white but they gradually turn pink because of a natural coloring in the food it eats.

 Greater flamingoes gather together in huge flocks of several thousand birds. They communicate with honking and cackling calls. Each bird has its own unique call.

 At the start of the breeding season, flamingoes put on a mating display. They stretch their necks upward, preen their feathers and march around in groups.

 The female flamingo lays a single egg on a mound of mud above the water. After hatching, the chicks are gathered into a group and looked after by several adults to keep them safe from predators.

Fact file

Lives: Southern Europe, Africa, Madagascar, Middle East and parts of Asia

Habitat: Shallow saltwater lakes and lagoons

Length: 4–4¾ ft (1.2–1.45 m)

Wingspan: 4½–5¼ ft (1.4–1.65 m)

Weight: 4½–9 lb (2.1–4.1 kg)

Lifespan: 50 years

Diet: Crustaceans, mollusks, worms, plants, algae

Great spotted woodpecker

Dendrocopos major

- The wormlike beetle grubs that live in tree trunks and branches are what the woodpecker likes to eat. To reach them, it hammers into the wood with its long beak.

- The woodpecker slams its beak into wood with enormous force. A springy joint at the base of its beak helps to absorb the shock.

- The great spotted woodpecker can drill a hole 4 in (10 cm) deep in the wood. It picks up the grubs inside with the tip of its tongue, which is covered in sticky bristles.

- The woodpecker's tongue can stretch 1½ in (4 cm) beyond the tip of its beak. But most of the time, it stays coiled up inside the back of its skull.

- Each of the woodpecker's feet has two forward-facing toes and two backward-facing toes. This gives it a strong grip for holding onto upright tree trunks.

- Great spotted woodpeckers tap out signals to each other by drumming on dead, hollow wood. They can drum at up to 16 beats per second.

- Together, the male and female woodpecker hollow out a nest hole high up in a tree trunk. The hole can be 14 in (35 cm) deep, with room for up to six chicks.

Fact file

Lives: Europe and Asia

Habitat: Woodland and forest

Length: 8–9½ in (20–24 cm)

Wingspan: 13¼–15¼ in (34–39 cm)

Weight: 2½–3½oz (66–98 g)

Lifespan: 11 years

Diet: Beetle grubs, spiders, insects, seeds, nuts, berries

Blue-winged kookaburra

Dacelo leachii

The Wiradjuri people from southeastern Australia gave this bird its name. *Kookaburra* sounds like the bird's loud, chuckling call.

Kookaburras live in families of up to twelve birds. The young help their parents to look after the eggs and new chicks, and to defend their territory.

The kookaburra sits motionless on a tree branch and waits for prey. It swoops down to grab the victim in its jaw, then flies back to its perch and bashes the prey on the branch to kill it.

Fact file

Lives: Northern Australia and southern New Guinea

Habitat: Open forest and woodland

Length: 15–16 in (38–41 cm)

Wingspan: 25½–28 in (65–72 cm)

Weight: 9–13 oz (250–370 g)

Lifespan: 10 years

Diet: Insects, reptiles, frogs, mammals, spiders, birds, fish, earthworms

Kookaburras do not drink much water. Instead, they get most of the liquid they need from the food they eat.

Newly hatched chicks have hooked beaks, which they use in fights with each other. The smallest chick often gets pushed out of the nest.

Kookaburra fledgings don't leave the nest as soon as they can fly. They stay for up to 13 weeks and are still fed by their parents during that time.

Peregrine falcon

Falco peregrinus

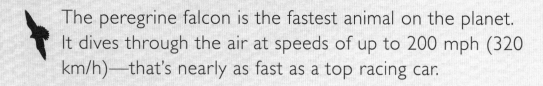

- The peregrine falcon is the fastest animal on the planet. It dives through the air at speeds of up to 200 mph (320 km/h)—that's nearly as fast as a top racing car.

- The speeding falcon swoops down on other birds in flight. It smashes into its prey feetfirst, killing it in an instant. The falcon's superfast dive is called a stoop.

- The air rushing into a diving falcon's nose moves so fast that it could burst the bird's lungs. Bony lumps inside its nostrils slow the air down to a safer speed.

- A transparent third eyelid slides sideways across the falcon's eye during its stoop. This protects it from dust and rain.

- The peregrine hunts anything from hummingbirds to pheasants. In cities, it likes to eat pigeons.

- The falcon nests on a ledge on a steep cliff. High up on the cliffside, it has a clear view of flocks of birds below.

- In cities, these deadly hunters nest on the windowsills of tall skyscrapers and look out for pigeons to eat.

Fact file

Lives: Worldwide

Habitat: Everywhere except
  rainforest and cold polar regions

Length: 13¾–20 in (35–51 cm)

Wingspan: 31–45 in (79–114 cm)

Weight: 1–3½ lb (0.41–1.6 kg)

Lifespan: 13 years

Diet: Birds, mammals, reptiles, insects

Victoria crowned pigeon

Goura victoria

 This colorful bird is the largest pigeon in the world. It is at least twice the size of the gray pigeons that live in towns.

 Victoria crowned pigeons strut around in small groups on the ground, looking for food. They search for soft, ripe fruits that have fallen from the trees. Sometimes they eat seeds and insects too.

 The pigeons flutter to the trees for safety when a predator approaches. The birds call to each other from their leafy perches. Their deep, whooping sounds tell each other where they are.

Fact file

Lives: New Guinea

Habitat: Swamp and forest

Length: 26–29½ in (66–75 cm)

Wingspan: 31½ in (80 cm)

Weight: 5 lb (2.4 kg)

Lifespan: Unknown

Diet: Fallen fruit, seeds, insects

Males compete with each other in the breeding season. They puff up their purple breasts, lift their wings, and dash at each other. They seldom collide because one of them usually runs away.

During the breeding season, tougher males chase away the weaker ones. They perform a bowing dance for the females and waggle their fanned tails.

The female pigeon lays one egg in a nest built in the trees. She cares for her chick for about 12 weeks.

Resplendent quetzal

Pharomachrus mocinno

This brightly colored bird is named after Quetzalcoatl, the Aztec god of the wind. A legend says that the god took the shape of a snake with beautiful feathers.

The male quetzal has an extra-long, shimmering tail called a streamer. This can be twice as long as the rest of his body.

The resplendent quetzal has short, rounded wings and doesn't fly further than 300 ft (100 m) at a time. Instead, the bird flaps around between fruit trees.

The quetzal often eats the berries of laurel trees. The seeds pass through its body and out in its droppings. They sprout, take root, and grow into new trees.

When the quetzal cannot find any fruit to feed on, it swoops down on small animals on the forest floor. It flies back up to the trees, eating its catch on the way.

The quetzel's feet are not suited to walking on the ground but are good for gripping onto branches. Each foot has two toes that face forward and two toes that face backward.

Fact file

Lives: Mexico and Central America

Habitat: Humid evergreen forest

Length: 14–15¾ in (36–40 cm)

Wingspan: 15¾ in (40 cm)

Weight: 6–7½ oz (180–210 g)

Lifespan: 3–10 years

Diet: Fruit, insects, snails, frogs, reptiles

Bald eagle

Haliaeetus leucocephalus

The bald eagle is not actually bald. Its head is covered in white feathers. The name comes from *balde*, an old word for *white*.

Sometimes the bald eagle hunts for fish or other animals, but usually it prefers to steal food from smaller birds of prey, or even from other bald eagles.

Bald eagles pair for life. They live in old trees, often taking over a nest that has been used by other eagles.

The nests of bald eagles are some of the biggest in the world. The largest is 8 ft (2½ m) deep and weighs 6,000 lb (3 tons).

Fact file

Lives: North America

Habitat: Wooded areas near rivers, lakes, or coasts

Length: 27½–37¾ in (70–96 cm)

Wingspan: 6–8 ft (1.8–2.4 m)

Weight: 7–13½ lb (3.2–6.2 kg)

Lifespan: 28 years

Diet: Fish, birds, reptiles, carrion

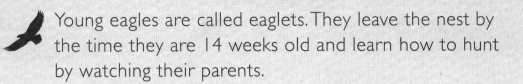 Young eagles are called eaglets. They leave the nest by the time they are 14 weeks old and learn how to hunt by watching their parents.

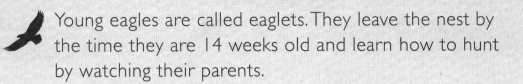 Bald eagles live for a long time. The oldest bald eagle reached the grand age of 38 years.

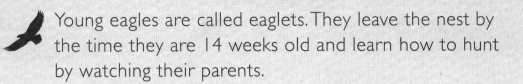 The bald eagle is the national emblem of the United States.

Gray crowned crane

Balearica regulorum

This impressive bird is named after the crest of golden feathers on its head. It uses the crest to show off to its mate in the breeding season.

Gray crowned cranes have long legs for wading in shallow water and striding through tall grass.

The cranes stamp on the ground as they walk to disturb insects in the grass, then snap up the food with their beaks.

A strong, backward-facing toe on each foot allows the crane to grip onto the branches of trees, even when it is sleeping.

Fact file

Lives: Eastern and southern Africa

Habitat: Grassland and wetland

Length: 3–3½ ft (1–1.1 m)

Wingspan: 6–6½ ft (1.8–2 m)

Weight: 6½–9 lb (3–4 kg)

Lifespan: 22 years

Diet: Grass, seeds, insects, small animals

These cranes pair for life. Mates perform elaborate dances of bows, strides, and jumps with wings stretched wide to impress each other.

51

Gouldian finch

Chloebia gouldiae

- This Australian songbird is also known as the rainbow finch because of the splashes of brilliant color in its plumage. Its face can be red, black, or orange.

- The finch chick has pearly blue lumps at the corners of its beak, which reflect light from outside. Their glow helps the parent birds to find the chick inside the dark nest.

- The Gouldian finch eats just over one-third of its own body weight in seeds every day.

- A female finch will choose a mate with the same head coloring as hers because he is a better match, and their chicks will have a better chance of survival.

- Finch chicks come out of the nest at the age of three weeks. They have dull green feathers and won't get their rainbow-colored adult plumage for at least four months.

Fact file

Lives: Australia

Habitat: Dry, open forest and woodland

Length: 6 in (15 cm)

Wingspan: 5½ in (14 cm)

Weight: ¼–½ oz (10.5–16 g)

Lifespan: 6 years

Diet: Grass seeds

Common raven

Corvus corax

 This big, all-black songbird is related to crows, magpies, and rooks, but is larger than any of them.

 The raven can produce more than 30 different calls. It can also mimic the cries of other birds.

 Ravens make high-pitched whistling noises by flapping their wings rapidly. Air rushing through their feathers makes the sound.

 The world's most famous ravens are kept at the Tower of London in England. Supersition says the fortress will collapse if the birds leave, so the ravenmaster sometimes clips their wings to stop them flying away.

Fact file

Lives: North America, Mexico, Europe, and Asia

Habitat: Most habitats

Length: 23–27 in (58–69 cm)

Wingspan: 47–59 in (120–150 cm)

Weight: 1¼–4½ lb (0.6–2 kg)

Lifespan: 15 years

Diet: Almost any food it can find

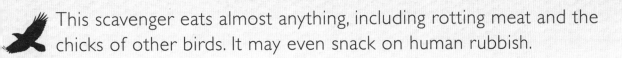 This scavenger eats almost anything, including rotting meat and the chicks of other birds. It may even snack on human rubbish.

These big birds like to roll around on anthills and let the ants swarm all over them. This "anting" is thought to keep the birds' feathers healthy.

Ravens are highly intelligent and playful. They are aerial acrobats, performing rolls and dives in the air.

The raven has an excellent memory for human faces. If a person comes too close to its nest, the bird will attack them every time it sees them.

Eastern bluebird

Sialia sialis

- The *blue* in the name *bluebird* comes from the color of its wings.

- The high-pitched call of the Eastern bluebird sounds as if it is saying "truly" over and over again.

- Eastern bluebirds are found in the eastern half of North America, from as far north as Canada all the way to Nicaragua in the south. They gather together in flocks of more than 100 birds.

- To attract a mate, the male bluebird flaps his wings while perched above the nest hole and goes in and out, carrying nesting material.

- The female bluebird builds the nest, but both parents share the care of the chicks when they are born. They take turns to feed them insects.

- Eastern bluebirds that live farther north and west tend to produce more eggs than bluebirds living in the east and south.

- Flying squirrels and chipmunks may take bluebird chicks from the nest. American kestrels and snakes prey on the adult birds.

Fact file

Lives: Eastern North America, Mexico, Central America, Bermuda

Habitat: Savannah, open forest

Length: 6–8¼ in (16–21 cm)

Wingspan: 10–12½ in (25–32 cm)

Weight: 1–1¼ oz (26–32 g)

Lifespan: 10 years

Diet: Insects, spiders, fruits, plants

Wandering albatross

Diomedea exulans

- The wandering albatross has the largest wingspan of any bird. Its outstretched wings measure up to 11½ ft (3.5 m) from tip to tip.

- The albatross glides on the ocean winds for days on end. It comes down to the surface only to catch food and to breed.

- A single albatross can fly all the way round Antarctica three times in one year, which is around 75,000 miles (120,000 km).

- At night, albatrosses hunt for the luminous squid that come to the surface to feed. By day, they hunt for other food.

- During the day the wandering albatross sleeps as it glides through the sky. It shuts down one half of its brain and dozes with one eye open, entering deep sleep for just a few seconds at a time.

Male and female albatrosses pair for life. They meet up on rocky islands in the Southern Ocean, where each female lays a single egg.

An albatross chick will not be ready to leave the nest until it is at least eight months old. All that time, its parents take turns to keep it fed.

Fact file

Lives: Southern Ocean and remote islands

Habitat: Ocean, nests on grassy slopes

Length: 3–4½ ft (1–1.4 m)

Wingspan: 8–11½ ft (2.5–3.5 m)

Weight: 14¾–26 lb (6.7–11.9 kg)

Lifespan: 50 years

Diet: Squid, octopus, fish, crustaceans

Common ostrich

Struthio camelus

 The ostrich is the biggest bird in the world, standing more than 6½ ft (2 m) tall.

 This high-speed runner is too heavy to fly, but it can race across the ground at a top speed of 43 mph (70 km/h). This is the fastest land speed of any bird.

 The flightless ostrich uses its outstretched wings to help steer itself and keep its balance.

 Ostrich eggs are the largest in the world. They weigh 3 lb (1.4 kg), which is around 20 times heavier than a hen's egg.

Fact file

Lives: Africa

Habitat: Semiarid savannah and desert

Length: 5¾–9 ft (1.75–2.75 m)

Wingspan: 6½ ft (2 m)

Weight: 198–344 lb (90–156 kg)

Lifespan: 40–45 years

Diet: Grass, leaves, seeds, insects, small animals

Female ostriches often lay their eggs in a shared nest, which is a shallow hollow scraped in the ground. Some nests contain more than 20 eggs.

Sometimes an ostrich will turn the eggs over with its beak. From far away, it looks as if the bird is burying its head in the sand.

Bee hummingbird

Mellisuga helenae

- This miniature bird is the tiniest in the world. It is around twice the size of a large bee.

- The hummingbird's wings are built to flap very fast. It is thought that they may beat more than 80 times per second.

- This tiny bird uses its tongue rather like a miniature pump to drain nectar from flowers. It can draw up 5–10 drops of nectar in 15 milliseconds.

- The high-speed wings allow the hummingbird to hover in midair in front of flowers, licking up nectar with its long, feathery tongue.

Fact file

Lives: Cuba and Isle of Pines

Habitat: Swamp and woodland

Length: 2–2¼ in (5.5–6 cm)

Wingspan: 1 in (3 cm)

Weight: less than ¼ oz (1.6–2.6 g)

Lifespan: 7 years

Diet: Nectar, small insects

To stay alive, the hummingbird has to consume its body weight in nectar and insects every day.

The eggs of the bee hummingbird are only ¼ in (7 mm) long, which is about the size of a pea.

Predators can't easily catch this little bird. It darts out of reach and can fly in all directions, even backward. It can also stop in midair.

Red crossbill

Loxia curvirostra

This small songbird gets its name from the shape of its beak. The tips do not meet but cross over each other, which enables the bird to extract seeds from pine cones.

The crossbill pushes its beak between the scales of pine cones. It removes the seed, using its tongue and the upper part of its beak, and skilfully removes the husk around the seed before swallowing it.

Male crossbills have red and gray plumage, but the females are green. These colors match the cones and needles of the pine trees where the birds live and help them to blend in.

Crossbill beaks aren't all exactly the same. The birds inherit their beak shapes from their parents. The shapes vary to suit the particular pine cones on which the birds feed.

Crossbills with the same beak shape make the same call. They flock together to search for their favorite variety of pine cone.

Crossbills breed early in the year, in time for the new crop of pine cones. If crops are especially good, the birds may breed for longer.

Fact file

Lives: Europe, Asia, North and Central America

Habitat: Coniferous forests

Length: 5½–8 in (14–20 cm)

Wingspan: 10 in (25 cm)

Weight: 1–2 oz (25–53 g)

Lifespan: 8 years

Diet: Seeds, buds, shoots, insects

Southern brown kiwi

Apteryx australis

Kiwis are flightless birds. Their wings are too small to see under their long, silky, furlike feathers.

The kiwi's beak is about a third as long as its body. It plunges its beak into soft soil or water to find prey, which it kills by banging it on the ground.

The kiwi hunts at night. It has very small eyes so uses the whiskers at the base of its beak to feel its way through the dense undergrowth.

Nostrils and sensors at the tip of the kiwi's beak allow it to detect prey underground. It finds the prey by smell and also by the vibrations it makes.

For their size, female kiwis lay the largest eggs of any bird. Each egg weighs one-sixth of the weight of the mother.

Kiwi eggs have very large yolks. The chicks don't absorb all the yolk until after they hatch, so they don't need to find food until they leave the nest 10 days later.

Fact file

Lives: New Zealand

Habitat: Forest and shrubland

Length: 18–21 in (45–54 cm)

Wingspan: 2 in (5 cm)

Weight: 3–8½ lb (1.4–3.9 kg)

Lifespan: 20 years

Diet: Insects, fallen fruit, seeds

Great hornbill

Buceros bicornis

The great hornbill gets its name from the horn, or casque, on its head.

Male hornbills have a darker casque than the females, and a red iris, which is the colored part of the eye. Females have a yellowish casque and a white iris.

The casque is hollow and spongy inside to make it light enough for flying.

During the breeding season, males sometimes bang casques together as they fly.

The hornbill hops along tree branches searching for food. It delicately plucks fruit with the tip of its beak.

The notched edges of the hornbill's beak make it a useful tool for tearing off bark to uncover the tasty insects underneath.

- The female builds a nest in a tree hollow and seals the opening with her droppings and those of her mate.

- The male hornbill keeps his mate supplied with food while she stays inside the nest to incubate the eggs.

- The newly hatched chick has no casque. It will take about five years to grow.

Fact file

Lives: Asia

Habitat: Evergreen forest

Length: 3–3¼ ft (0.95–1 m)

Wingspan: 5 ft (1.5 m)

Weight: 5–7½ lb (2.2–3.4 kg)

Lifespan: 35–40 years

Diet: Fruit, plants, insects

Common kingfisher

Alcedo atthis

- The common kingfisher goes hunting for fish along the banks of rivers. It perches about 6½ ft (2 m) above the surface, scanning for food in the clear water below.

- The kingfisher's eye has a droplet of red oil inside it. This helps to reduce the glare of sunlight on the water's surface.

- When it sees a fish, the kingfisher dives straight down into the water to grab the prey with its beak. It opens its wings to stop itself plunging further, then returns to the surface.

- The common kingfisher can see as well under the water as it does in the air. A transparent third eyelid covers each eye underwater, like swimming goggles.

- Sticklebacks are among the kingfisher's prey. These fish have backward-pointing spines on their bodies. The kingfisher eats them headfirst to stop the spines getting stuck in its throat.

- After a dive, the kingfisher has to dry out its wet feathers. It neatens them with its long beak, which is a quarter the length of its body.

- The male kingfisher gives the female a fish as a gift before mating.

Fact file

Lives: Europe, North Africa, Middle East and Asia

Habitat: Wooded areas near water

Length: 6–7 in (16–18 cm)

Wingspan: 9½ in (24 cm)

Weight: ¾–1½ oz (19–46 g)

Lifespan: 15 years

Diet: Fish, sometimes insects

Kakapo

Strigops habroptilus

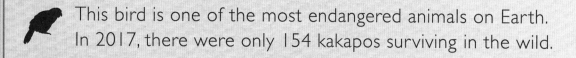 This bird is one of the most endangered animals on Earth. In 2017, there were only 154 kakapos surviving in the wild.

New Zealand has no natural mammal predators. However, in the 1800s, European settlers introduced cats, rats, and stoats, and these animals killed all the kakapos on the main islands.

The kakapo is the world's heaviest parrot. It has small wings and weak chest muscles, so it cannot fly.

This flightless bird hides away in bushes by day. It comes out to feed at night to keep safe from eagles and other natural predators.

The kakapo freezes like a statue when threatened by a predator. Its speckled plumage conceals it from birds that hunt by sight, but not from mammals that hunt by scent.

Male kakapos make low, booming calls all night to attract mates. They dig themselves a bowl-shaped hollow to make their booming even louder.

Fact file

Lives: New Zealand

Habitat: Mountain slopes

Length: 25 in (64 cm)

Wingspan: 31½ in (80 cm)

Weight: 2–6½ lb (0.95–3 kg)

Lifespan: 60 years or more

Diet: Most plant parts

Marabou stork

Leptoptilos crumenifer

- This stork's nickname is the "the undertaker bird." Its dark gray and black feathers, long, skinny legs, and white, fluffy chest make it look like a smartly dressed undertaker, who organizes funerals.

- The marabou stork soars high above the ground looking for—and smelling—the rotting remains of dead animals.

- The stork's massive beak is up to 14 in (35 cm) long. It can reach deep inside carcasses to pluck out meaty scraps.

- There are no feathers on the stork's head or neck because these would get dirty with blood and guts when it feeds.

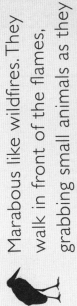 Marabous like wildfires. They walk in front of the flames, grabbing small animals as they escape from the burning grass.

 The male stork puffs up its throat pouch during courtship. It croaks and chatters, and rattles its bill.

Fact file

Lives: Africa

Habitat: Dry grassland and savannah near water, swamps

Length: 4–5 ft (1.2–1.5 m)

Wingspan: 7 ft (2.2 m)

Weight: 9–19½ lb (4–8.9 kg)

Lifespan: 25 years

Diet: Carrion, and any other food it can find

Budgerigar
Melopsittacus undulatus

The name of these small birds comes from the word *betcherrygah* in the Gamilaraay language of Australia. It translates as "good bird."

These little members of the parrot family have round swellings, called ceres, at the base of their beaks. The male's ceres are blue and the female's are brown.

Large flocks of budgerigars travel long distances to find fresh water to drink. They also follow the rainstorms that encourage grass to grow, which produces seeds to eat.

Aboriginal people knew that budgerigars could find sources of fresh water in the dry Australian Outback, so they followed the flocks to see where they went.

Fact file

Lives: Australia

Habitat: Open savannah, forest and desert

Length: 6¾–7 in (17–18 cm)

Wingspan: 20 in (30 cm)

Weight: 1 oz (26–29 g)

Lifespan: 15 years

Diet: Seeds

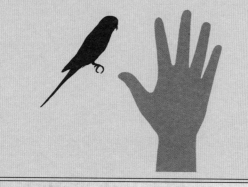

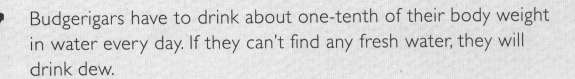

Budgerigars have to drink about one-tenth of their body weight in water every day. If they can't find any fresh water, they will drink dew.

Wild budgerigars are generally green and yellow. They have been bred in captivity to have many colors.

Both male and female budgerigars sing. The males can also learn to whistle and mimic other sounds, including human speech.

Indian peafowl

Pavo cristatus

A male peafowl is called a peacock and the female is known as a peahen. To impress the females, the peacock spreads out his 200 brilliantly colored tail feathers into a huge fan.

Peahens prefer males with the most shimmering eyespots on their tails. They also like peacocks with the widest tail fans. A large tail is a sign of a strong male that will produce healthy chicks.

Peacocks have shiny blue, green, and gold feathers on their neck and breast. Peahens are brown and gray and have shorter tails.

Birds see in color so a peahen can spot a peacock's bright tail against the undergrowth. Mammals that prey on peafowl don't detect color as well, so they may not notice the male.

Fact file

Lives: Indian subcontinent

Habitat: Open forest near water

Length: 3–7½ ft (0.9–2.3 m)

Wingspan: 2½–5 ft (0.8–1.6 m)

Weight: 6–13 lb (2.7–6 kg)

Lifespan: 25 years

Diet: Mainly plants, also insects, small reptiles and mammals

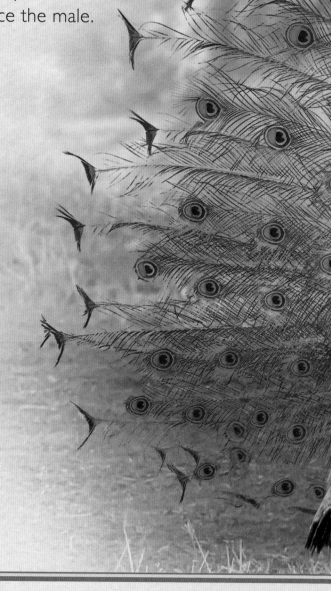

These big birds spend most of their time on the ground. They roost high up in trees at night, out of reach of predators such as big cats and wild dogs.

Peafowl shriek loudly when a predator approaches. Other nearby peafowl join win to pass on the message.

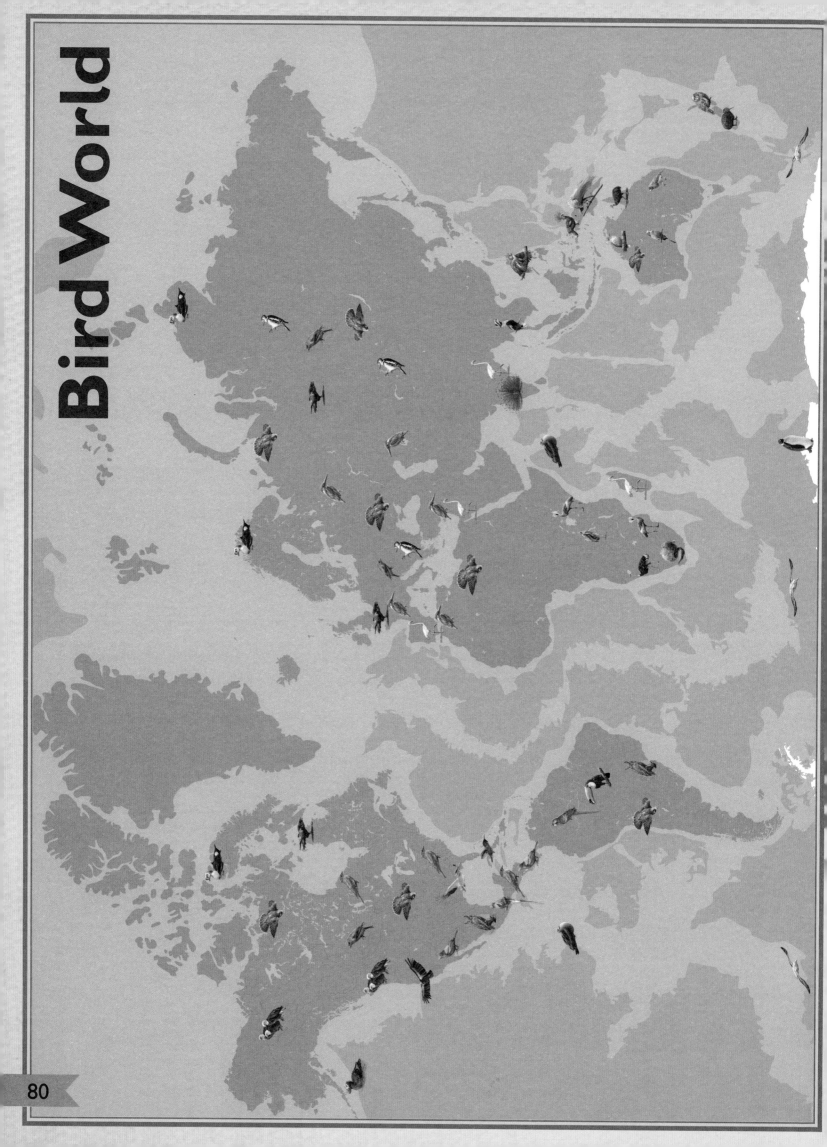

Bird World